The Dirty Sheep

'ir'

birds	blackbird

birch	dirty

thirsty	first

girl	third

chirped

The month was March. Winter was almost over. The buds were opening on the trees. The birds were singing again.

A blackbird was making a nest. It found some moss on the ground under a birch tree. It flew back to its nest with it.

The blackbird was putting the moss in the nest, when it saw a mound of wool on the ground.

The blackbird flew down to the wool and pecked it. The wool moved. Then it said, 'baa, baa, baa.'

The mound of wool was a sheep. It was a very dirty sheep. It was thirsty too. The blackbird wanted to help it.

The blackbird flew off to find Jelly and Bean. They were in the barn. The blackbird chirped at them to go to help the sheep.

Jelly and Bean took the dirty sheep to the water tub. She had a long drink of water.

Then they took her into the barn. She sat down on a bed of hay. She did not move all day.

Later three lambs were born. The first lamb was a girl. The second lamb was a boy. The third lamb was a girl.

The next day the blackbird went to see the lambs. Then it chirped the good news to all the animals in the farmyard.

Vowels:

ay/ai:	day hay again
ee/ea:	trees sheep three see Bean
i:	find
o:	almost over opening go
ew/oo:	flew news too
oo:	took wool good
ow/ou:	down found ground mound
ar:	March barn farmyard
er:	winter over under water later
ir:	birds blackbird birch first dirty thirsty girl third chirped
or:	born
er/ear:	her
aw/al:	saw almost all
-y:	very Jelly dirty thirsty

Verbs:

-ed verbs:	moved chirped pecked wanted
Others:	was were found flew saw said had did went took sat

Exceptions: water move lambs some they month boy